Quick Guide VII:
A Top-notch, Sales-Relationships, Account Management Template

I0483965

Number 7 in a series of articles by

Paul C Burr PhD

http://paulcburr.com/

Acknowledgements

Professor John S Ditch

Kelly Scales, Management Consultant and
Entrepreneur

Penelope Walsh, Writer and Book Editor

Business Booklets by the Author

Quick Guide: How Top Salespeople Sell

*Quick Guide II: How to Spot, Mimic and Become a Top
Salesperson*

*Quick Guide III: How to Bridge the Pillars of Successful
Business Relationships*

*Quick Guide IV: A Scorecard that Accounts for
Mindfulness in Business*

*Quick Guide V: How to Apply Mindfulness to Business
Relationships*

Quick Guide VI: How to Sell Coaching

Other Books and Booklets by the Author

*For The Love of Lilith & How to Put Love into Practice
(and Non-attach Yourself to It)*

The Mystique to the Game of Life (and Unrequited Love)

Defrag your Soul

2012: a twist in the tail - a novel

Learn to Love & Be Loved in Return

Contents

Preface

This booklet, in common with each of my other *Quick Guides to Business*, can be read quickly, in less than an hour.

The contents embody and reflect my research, consulting, direct selling and coaching within global corporations over a twenty year period. The companies I worked directly for, or in a freelance capacity with, include: IBM, Cisco, Accenture, Xerox, Microsoft, American Express, Standard Chartered, BP and Reckitt Benckiser. During this period I've had the privilege to meet, work with and coach hundreds of top performers worldwide.

When I use the word, 'you', I mean 'you', 'me', 'we', 'us'... anyone.

Paul C Burr

January 2015

The Whys and Wherefores

Virtually all of the large corporations I've worked with have each spent millions of dollars ($US) installing customised sales systems and account management processes. This booklet will give you a snapshot of the core wisdom you need to adopt a 'best-practice' account management system for a few pounds (£UK) or dollars ($US).

I have designed a number of sales campaign planning and management systems for complex B2B organisational relationships, i.e. several sales and sales support people selling to a variety of individuals in the same client organisation.

I have applied this experience to design a series of single-page templates that combine to create an overall account management template for both a large and medium sized sales organisation. I have pared everything down to the core and most important wisdom necessary to facilitate a highly effective B2B relationships-based account management process.

If knowledge is intelligible information then wisdom is actionable knowledge. And the wisdom shared in any account management system needs to be easily accessible, by those with authority, to inform decisions and act more wisely.

Why is effective account management so important?

I remember, when in corporate sales, that many customers found (what seemed a never ending) change of customer facing people (e.g. salespeople, systems engineering, customer administration) a frustration. Upon walking into a 'new' account, I'd quite often hear the mirthful phrase, "Oh, are you the latest salesperson we have to educate on how to do business with us?"

When such changeovers take place, it can take a newcomer several months to establish a healthy level of trust (in his/her capability and integrity) with their 'new' client. First impressions (for example, that you've done your homework on your organisations' relationship with the client) count. Without an effective account management process, this period of 'building trust' can take a lot longer. And trust is paramount because...

'Lack of trust in the sales relationship' is the single biggest factor for a customer to move to another supplier.

Likewise, in complex B2B relationships, a single client might meet several salespeople from the same organisation. Imagine their frustration meeting a series of 'new' salespeople who have little or no prior knowledge of their sales organisation's relationship history (or who else in their sales organisation is engaging currently) with that individual.

Changes in personnel are not always planned for either. I recall being asked to stand in for a fellow salesperson who had suddenly fallen seriously ill. He was coming to the close of a long sales campaign worth millions of pounds (£UK). His client organisation was going to make its decision within three to four weeks and I had difficulty getting into the diaries of some of its key decision makers. I needed to get up to speed as quickly as possible from the incumbent systems engineers and various people with experience of dealing with the client. I wanted to understand the areas of value that the client's key decision makers personally placed upon doing business with my company and my competitors. If all the information in the following template had been made available to me in one repository, it would have saved me and my company a lot of time, money (and grief).

So far I've discussed the downside of NOT having an institutional account management system. Before I get to the upside there exist...

Two Critical Success Factors:

1. **Buy-in:** To make any sales-management system work properly, the sales-force need to 'buy in' to it. It needs to be quick, easy to build and maintain, with minimal use of one of salespeople's most precious assets, time! An hour spent 'filling in forms' is an hour not selling.

2. **Truth:** Such a system is only of value if it based on truth. Walking into a client's office with

misinformation could be more damaging than walking in with no information at all. Yet there's a bigger danger as to why account management systems often include 'economies of truth'. This can happen when they are used as management reporting tools and there exists a lack of trust between the sales-force and the management hierarchy.

Case Study: Lack of Trust Leads to a Lack of Truth, i.e. Game-playing

I once worked with an organisation where sales-support resource requests for 'top-tier' sales campaigns, worth more than a certain value and forecasted at more than a 50% chance of winning, came under close management scrutiny. The salesperson running such campaigns was obliged to participate in a series of management reviews to account for the sales-support resources and budget requested to win their campaign.

These reviews were considered onerous and unnecessary by the sales-force. Many of the top salespeople 'played' the system by keeping campaign forecasts just below the 'review-trigger-value' levels with a '40% likelihood'. Top performers with a good track record in sales had no problem attracting the top support people, who naturally wanted to be associated with success. So, with little advance warning, the top salespeople would lobby for the resources needed by informing management that there was no time for reviews.

In the meantime, moderate performing salespeople were often tempted to pitch on the high side for resources in order to grab management's attention.

Result: management spent most of its time reviewing misinformation, whilst still 'in-fighting' for resources available. The system thus failed to meets its objectives of making best use of limited resources, as management had very little 'truth' on its review books. And, management was obliged to comply with last minute requests because it relied very highly upon the top salespeople to bring in the vast majority (>80%) of sales revenue.

Note, the issue in this specific organisation was two-fold...

1. Management was perceived as asking for unnecessary information. But...
2. The key underlying issue was a lack of trust between management and salespeople. Neither party trusted the other to make the right call for limited sales resources.

The problem was resolved by one or two 'out-of-the-box' thinking managers who set up peer-to-peer reviews in which sales teams managed resource allocation for themselves. Alas, this peer-evaluation approach met a lot of resistance because of the organisation's hierarchically-regimented culture (end).

The Upside

An efficient sales account management system rooted in truth can create a significant benefit to sales and cost management.

1. Newcomers to, and reviewers of, a complex account relationship get a solid view of the relationship opportunities and issues faced, from both an intellectual and emotional perspective.
2. The selling organisation creates and maintains a reassuring perception by the client when its representatives appear consistently prepared and informed.
3. Key client relationships are monitored carefully, especially for any changes in perception.
4. Better informed judgements can be made on the resourcing and actions required to win each sales campaign.
5. Direct and onward costs, of processing misinformation or lack of information about a client and its key decision makers, are obviated.

Before we get on with the Template (suite) itself, let us start categorising different individual client relationships according to their power, influence and wisdom.

———

Relationships: the First and Last of All Selling

If you only complete one exercise from this booklet, complete this one.

When you sell a product or service into an organisation, you 'meet' four categories of people. The categories are not necessarily exclusive of one another.

Four Categories of People Who Help/Hinder Selling

1. Those with the *power of veto*, including yourself, who can stop you winning your sales campaign.
2. Those who *sway influence* over those who have the power of veto.
3. Those who have expertise or experience in *making change happen*, especially customer-oriented change, in your client organisation.
4. Those who have *experience in selling*...
   a. what you're selling and/or
   b. to whom you are selling.

The first piece of advice is simple...

When no-one with the power of veto wants to stop you from selling, including yourself, then you cannot fail. You succeed.

Focus your relationship strategies, first and foremost, on those with the power of veto.

Positional authority does not imply that an individual will exercise their power of veto. I have met many executives, with budgetary authority, who early on in a sales campaign have implied that they would be pleased to buy the products and services I was selling. In reality, what they really meant was, *"I'll be pleased to sign off a recommendation from my staff in your favour but I will not veto a recommendation for your competitor"*.

I 'cut my teeth' in selling to a department of senior mathematicians and statisticians, none of who had much interest in the technicalities of IT products and services, including the IT Director. When push came to shove, all IT investment decisions were 'as recommended' by a technical operations manager who resided in a lowly basement office. I made especially sure that I was always in tune with his needs and wants from a supplier. Of all those with the power of veto, the technical operations manager, in this instance, was the 'most powerful' decision maker.

Anyone whose job, function or power has the potential to be affected, positively or negatively, by the product or service you are selling will take an interest and thus may well have some sway of influence.

Case Study: One Secret of a Salesperson Who Consistently Made Several Hundred Percent of Sales Targets

Speaking of 'influence', this leads me to a 'gem' given to me by a Middle-Eastern sales representative, of a global IT supplier, who consistently over-achieved his sales targets by several hundred percent.

I was conducting research into what key sales top performers do differently from moderate performers.

I was about to take this top-performing salesperson through a five page questionnaire when he stopped me immediately.

"Paul," he interrupted politely, "do you want to take me through your questionnaire or, given we only have limited time, would you like to know what I do that my colleagues don't do?"

I closed the questionnaire; with pen in hand, I opened my note pad to a fresh clean page and nodded, "Please tell me!"

"When I first research and start with a new account, I often avoid the IT department as much as I can. Instead I look for executives who have instigated major, ideally 'customer-centric', change in my client's organisation. I seek out the 'movers and shakers' from news reports, trade journals and the internet.

Two things: these people...

1. ...Know how to influence the Board of the organisation and carry significant influence.
2. ...Are ambitious 'movers and shakers'. They thrive on making change happen. If I have something significant and tenable to offer the client's organisation, they will often want to be involved as a sponsor, programme manager or at least as an advisor.

So I ask them for a short meeting – for which my reason is simple. I say something direct, like, 'If I'm not talking to you then I'm not doing my job properly'.

By and large, they are happy to see me."

*** End of Case Study ***

The above case study emphasises the importance a 'mover and shaker' can play as an ally (or foe) to your sales campaigns. They will fall under Category 1 or 2 – and Categories 3 and 4.

Speaking of Category 4, those who have *experience,* I learnt the most about selling by shadowing wise salespeople on client calls, when I first started 'corporate life' with IBM. I copied their behaviour patterns and memorised the little nuances they had for dealing with awkward questions. For instance...

Case Study Example: Handling Sales Objections

I 'shadow-called' with a senior sales representative (and my mentor) selling IBM mainframe solutions to a corporate client. One of my mentor's competitors was another 'IBMer' selling small systems solutions. At the start of the meeting, the customer took me (the trainee) completely by surprise.

The customers first words were, "I've already had an IBM colleague of yours recommending the impressive System 'XX'. Why have you come to see me?"

My first reaction was panic. I thought, "Help. How does one IBM salesperson take on another?"

My senior colleague nodded confidently and spoke, "And it is an impressive system. So before we discover which options are open to you, can you tell me what you liked about the System XX?"

I was taught in a nutshell, the best way to handle an objection was to seek clarity about what the client thinks and feels by, first of all, asking a question. And before asking the question, you infer that you have heard what you think the client's objection is all about. In this case, the client had expressed confusion – but was he genuinely confused or was he having a bit of fun (as we often do in UK) with us.

We soon got down to the bottom of it. It was a bit of both: confusion and humour. The sales call progressed well thereon (end).

Senior sales-mentors helped me enormously to cut short the 'mostly errors from trial' period that IBM allowed me during my early months in sales. Thirty years on, we remain good pals. Our bond can never be broken.

Top salespeople, the top 10-20%, form an organisation's Category 4 people. Others, especially the up-and-coming rising stars, copy them. Top performers can have a great influence over the rest of an organisation's sales-force – especially when their wisdom is channelled proactively to everyone. I've worked with sales management teams in recent years to automate and accelerate this wisdom-transfer process – to raise sales performance across the whole organisation.

———

Summarised Business Scorecard

The scorecard that follows summarises the actions you take, and what's driving these actions, to forge superior relationships within your client organisation. Moreover, it summarises where you, the salesperson, are and how well you equip yourself to succeed.

Summarised (Mindfulness) Scorecard

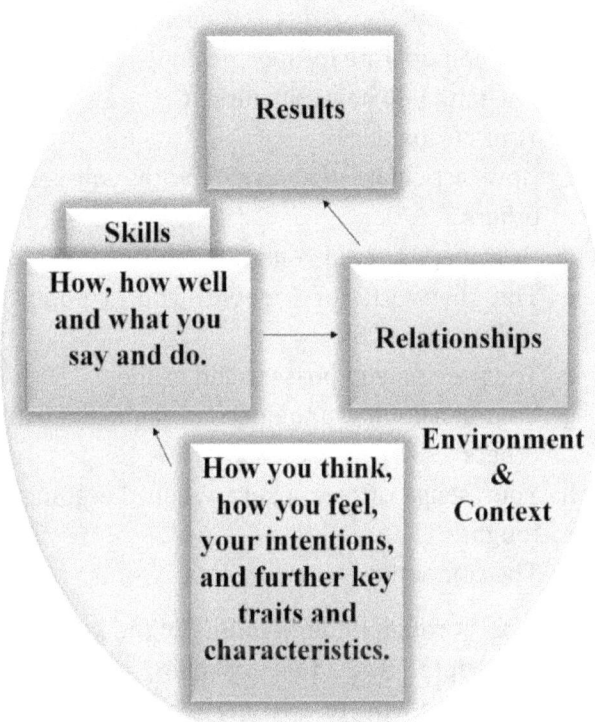

In a nutshell...
1. You achieve superior sales results by forging superior client relationships.
2. You forge superior relationships by how, how well and what, you say and do.
3. How well you say and do things is influenced by your skills, but more fundamentally...

4. What you say and do is influenced by how you think, how you feel, and your intentions.
5. How you think and feel, and your intentions, are influenced by *key traits*, characteristics and the context you operate in. Specifically:
    a. The faith you have in yourself
    b. Your curiosity
    c. How articulate you are – with yourself and others
    d. How inspirational you are
    e. The network of people you co-opt and collaborate with
    f. The passion you possess and exude
    g. Your sensibility to the needs, wants and fears of others
    h. Your sense of composure when the going gets tough
    i. The competitive environment

For a more thorough understanding of the *key traits* of top salespeople and the *business (mindfulness) scorecard*, I refer you to two earlier booklets in this series...

- *Quick Guide II – How to Spot, Mimic and Become a Top Salesperson*
- *Quick Guide IV – A Scorecard that Accounts for Mindfulness in Business*

———

Client Organisation Profile

Client:

Nature of Businesses they are in or will be in:
Financials:
No of Employees:
Structure:

Client CEO's Business Drivers:
- Cost Down

- Revenue/Market Share Up

- Agility/Speed

- Security

- Governance

- Product/Service/Cost Leadership

- Other (eg Technology, New Business Models)

Relevant Industry Trends

Client's Customers' Demands

Change – within and without

Personal Issues and Interests:

Competition/Other Services Used:
Any Other Points to Note:

Each client organisation is allocated at least one overarching *Profile Page*. A corporate client may warrant several *Client Organisation Profile Pages* for each of its divisions, regions, countries of operation and so on.

The completion of the *Client Organisation Profile Page* is fairly self explanatory. (You can source a lot of the information these days directly from the internet, as well as company reports, marketing collateral and providers of corporate profiling services.) Study the blank pro-forma on the preceding page.

Notes regarding...

Structure(s):

When recording the structure of your client's organisation focus on its physical structure, its financial structure (e.g. cost centres, profit centres) and its decision making structure (e.g. centralised, decentralised, budgetary limits).

Client CEO's Business Drivers:

I focus on the client-CEO's personal business drivers because any proposals that support their aspirations will naturally carry favour. The summarised list is research based. For a more thorough understanding of what motivates a CEO, I refer you to subsections *What CEOs value* and *What CEOs fear* from the first booklet in this series, *Quick Guide: How Top Salespeople Sell.*

Competitive/Other Services Used:

Complete a Purchase History profile (see next section) for each major competitive (or in-house) product or service used.

———

Purchase History – Value Contribution to Date

Complete a Purchase History for each relevant product or service used (or being considered) by the client. Include all own, competitive and in-house solutions.

Purchase History:

Products/Services Purchased:	
Revenue Value:	Date Started: Date Ended:
Reasons for Buying:	

Level of Perceived Overall Value Contribution: ....
Circle one of the below
1. Opposer: unwilling/unlikely to choose us as a supplier
2. Open-minded: indifferent/neutral about or fairly loyal toward buying from us
3. Advocate: highly likely, if not committed, to choose us as a supplier

Reasons for above:

Major "plus" factors influencing context of our relationship (what's going well) and actions to build upon these further:

Major issues/problems inhibiting our opportunities (what's not going well), what do we want instead and how do we get it?

The focus of the Purchase History is to assess the client's overall perception of value for money between your products/services and alternative solutions.

I use differing approaches to each of the **three types of customer-perspectives...**

1. *Opposer - unwilling/unlikely to choose us as a supplier*: are averse, if not repulsed, to buying from you or your company. Any information you give them, they will use ('game-play') against you. The approach is to arrest any 'game playing'; put an end to any deceit and get the truth on the table, and hopefully move the client up to become at least open-minded.

   If you do not get out of the 'game playing', i.e. you attempt to 'play the game' yourself, you will probably end up worsening the 'opposer's' view of you and increase their resolve to defeat you.

Case Study: My 'Opposer', Senior Operations Manager

I was selling large IT solutions to a major organisation based in London. I hadn't been selling to this particular client for long when I noticed I had a huge rearguard exposure to protect a large order placed with my employer before I became the client's salesperson.

It took me two or three months to find out that my selling was being undermined by an important individual in the client-organisation's middle management. I resorted to 'game playing' myself with this individual. I would sell above and below his station. I avoided selling to him directly or giving him any information about what I was doing or to whom I was selling in his organisation.

Later, whilst my 'opposer' was away on vacation, I closed a big deal quickly and had it signed off by his stand-in. When I got back from a subsequent vacation of my own, I found that my competitors had been awarded a quick piece of business which allowed them to get their foot in the client's door for the first time. This type of game-playing ('sales skirmishes') went on for a year or so.

Things came to a head one day and I invited my 'opposer' out for a light business meal. I put my cards on the table. I told him of my feelings about our relationship and asked him directly if he had a problem with me personally or the company I worked for. He answered that it was mainly the latter case; he disliked the company I worked for intensely, and also felt that I had made insufficient effort to work with him in the first place. I accepted his criticism unconditionally.

From that day on, we started to put our trust in one another and within two or three months we got along fine. My client demonstrated 'open-mindedness' (see next approach) about any proposals I put forward - which was all that I could ask for, given the circumstances (end).

2. ***Open-minded - indifferent/neutral about or fairly loyal toward buying from us:*** You are in a fair fight. This is about seeking/agreeing all the sources of value unique to you, seeking and handling all the objections against you, and ultimately inspiring the customer to decide in your favour. (For a more thorough understanding of how top salespeople inspire customers, I refer you to *Quick Guide: How Top Salespeople Sell*.)

3. ***Advocate - highly likely, if not committed, to choose us as a supplier:*** will share their fears with you and will value the same honesty from you. There's no game-playing involved. The better you equip them, the better they are at selling your solution inside their organisation for you.

———

Relationship Statuses

Relationship Statuses

Key contact and title	Date of assessment	Role in Buying Process & Value Orientation Power of 1. Veto er 2. Sway 3. Change maker 4. Expert	Partnership, Relationship, Intellectual Property or Transactional	Personal Disposal Toward Us 1. Opposer 2. Open-minded 3. Advocate	What can we do/offer that this person will value? Annotate in brackets with: N – Not unique S – Strength D – Unique differentiator	What impact will the differentiators have on the client's business: processes, people, personal agenda, and customers?

This section records the nub of your prospect of successful selling. It contrasts the key stakeholders' dispositions towards buying from you, to inform the strategies you develop to further your value-strengths and defend your value-weaknesses against competition.

Once again, the column headings are fairly self explanatory. (Third column, first sub-column) I have already covered the four roles of *Power of Veto, Sway of Influence, Change Makers and Experts* in the section, *Relationships: the First and Last of All Selling.*

In the third column, second sub-column, I introduce the *Customer Value Orientation Matrix* (see next page) to help you further analyse and develop sources of value toward key stakeholders, and avoid sources of value they consider inappropriate (always check through inquiry though).

Customer Value Orientation Matrix

The matrix informs us that customer value can have intellectual and/or emotional dimensions, or neither. Let's start with the neither...

1. *Transactional:* In this quadrant the individual client tends to place value for money upon the cost of the product and service quality they are buying and little or nothing more. In a commodity sale, given the minimum criteria of quality required, the client will make their decision typically on the lowest cost supplier. They attach neither emotional nor intellectual value on doing business with one vendor over another.

2. *Intellectual:* Over and above product and service quality some clients will value a vendor's

intellectual property, i.e. their expertise, wisdom, data and/or whom they know.

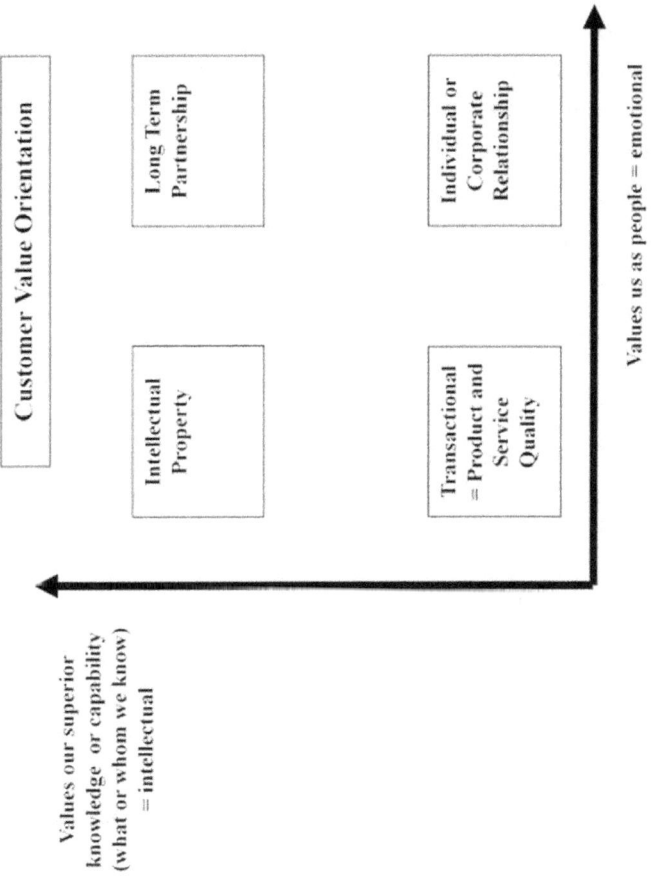

I once sold worldwide best-practice research to IT Directors as part of a private club subscription. Over and above the value of accessing millions of pounds (£UK) of research, at a small fraction of the cost, many members joined to meet their peers face-to-face. They met informally on a regular basis to discuss 'hot topics' of their own choice. Members would share insights into major IT management issues. If nothing more, members shared solace amongst themselves that they all struggled with the same management issues.

3. **_Emotional:_** In the UK, themes such as 'Buy British' or 'our Customer Support is based in the UK' continue to carry favour with some clients.

I have sold millions of pounds (£UK) worth of contracts by asking the client if they would help me to make or overachieve my sales targets at year end. In each case, I had a very close and trusting relationship with the client. They were willing and happy to bring forward the business simply because I asked for it.

Case Study: A Surprise and Wonderful Contract of Thanks

I led a sales and installation project of a huge network of Personal Computers (PCs) to facilitate a new customer service support system for a UK national corporate client. My organisation was awarded Phase 1 of a two phase project. I was told informally that Phase 2 would probably be awarded to a competitor whose product was some 40% cheaper.

The client valued my organisation's technical know-how and I assembled a top support team to make sure that Phase 1 was commissioned on time and within budget. By the end of our contract, the customer was delighted.

I managed to persuade my management to keep the support team in place, even though our contract for Phase 1 had been fulfilled. I was determined to ensure the complete project was a success. Specifically, I did not attempt to negotiate anything in return for this 'extra resource' commitment.

Phase 2 got underway. About half way through and to my complete surprise, I was awarded a further £3M worth of unexpected business. The client-sponsor was "simply delighted" with my organisation's commitment to the project overall regardless that a competitor was supposed to be supplying the hardware for Phase 2. This was the client-sponsor's way of saying "thank you" (end).

4. *Partnership:* When a client valucs doing business with you from both an intellectual and emotional basis, you have the potential to forge a partnership.

A business partnership is to all intensive purposes a marriage between your organisation and your client. You'll sit together at a common 'planning table'. Collectively you'll form 'one team'. You and your client's organisation will ideally have a matching *hierarchy of values.*

Case Study: A Mismatch in Values

I once engaged with a global apparel manufacturer to 'measure' the value its major retailer clients placed on the various products and services it offered. It sold prime marque products at premium prices. It was very successful but had a mismatch of values with one giant retailer in particular.

The retailer placed little or no value on the various add-on services the manufacturer provided, such as: local marketing campaigns, TV advertising, electronic tagging, in-store merchandising and so on. The retailer's mentality was 'stack-em-high, sell-em-cheap'; a complete contrast to prime-product retailing. The retailer was more interested in selling the manufacturer's 'bin-ends' and 'seconds'. And so a deal was eventually cut but the prospect of a partnership never came to fruition. The retailer's view of all suppliers was totally *Transactional* (end).

> The partnership will sustain when it is built on pillars of passion, resonance, security and creativity. The pillars are cemented in trust and as long as their bedrock is sound, pillars can crumble and be rebuilt.

For more information on forging and sustaining business relationship I refer you to two earlier booklets in this series...

- *Quick Guide III – How to Bridge the Pillars of Successful Business Relationships*
- *Quick Guide V – How to Apply Mindfulness to Business Relationships*

26

Columns 4 and 5 in the *Relationship Statuses* page are completed through inquiry, determination and measurement, in the heart and mind of the client, of all the sources of value by which you can differentiate yourself from competition. The *Customer Value Orientation* will guide your focus on different aspects (quadrants) of customer value. The disposition of the client (oppose, neutral or advocate) will inform you of the most appropriate approach by which to deal with each individual. The power the client has in the decision making process (veto, influencer, expert) will prompt you to prioritise where and with whom you focus your time and energy.

———

Customer Weighted Product/Service Value Opportunity Matrix

The ...*Value Opportunity Matrix* (see overleaf) applies to...

1. **Large complex relationships** where the vendor is selling multiple products and services to multiple locations, divisions, or buying centres within a single client. **Or..**,

2. It can be used to gauge where to focus your effort **across the whole sales territory** you are responsible for.

Customer Weighted Product/Service Value by Geography - Opportunity Matrix

Value Scores: 1 = not at all, 2 = very low, 3 = low, 4 = average, 5 = high, 6 = very high, 7 = paramount Customer Region/Dept:	Product/Service A Value to....				B	C	D......
	Customer: C = (1-7)	Us: U = (1-7)	Total: T = C^2U	Index %age: $I = T * \frac{100}{343}$			
A	5	4	100	29			
B	6	2	72	21			
C	2	6	24	7			
D	7	1	49	14			
E	1	7	7	2			
F	7	7	343 (max)	100			
G							
H...							

28

Ostensibly, you assign a value of 1 to 7 that each customer department/buying-centre places on each product and service you are considering selling to it. You assign the value of the sale, from 1 to 7, to your own organisation. I like to use the weighting of multiplying the square of the customer value (C) by the value to value to my own organisation (U).

For example consider the row, Customer Region/Department A and column, Product/Service A, in the illustration above.

Customer value, C = 5 (You client places a 'high value' on the benefits of buying A)

Vendor value, U = 4 (Your organisation places an 'average value' to the contract of selling A)

Total weighted value, $T=C^2U$ = 5x5x4 = 100, out of a maximum score of 343 (=7x7x7), and thus has an index of 29% (= T x100/343).

I prefer to weight the customer value by squaring its value but you can use any multiplier you prefer (for example: T =CU, C^3U and so on) as long as you are consistent.

The resultant chart tots up a matrix of relative 'measures' to gauge where, with whom, and on what to focus your sales resources. It is not absolute. There may be other reasons on the why and where you focus your sales. The chart is intended as a guide to maximise the perceived value opportunity you bring across the breadth and depth of your client base with all your products and services.

_____

Closing Notes

The focus of this, and all my booklets in this series, is to found your selling in truth and value. It's not about right and wrong, it's about what works and doesn't work in the heart and mind of the client, your management, your sales support people, your delivery team and you. Problems (dare I say "only") occur when these views are out of synch.

The completed suite of charts and templates will give you, your team, and anyone involved in your sales and delivery campaigns, a common basis to understand what it is your selling, how you are selling, to whom you are selling and why. It will save you significant time in management and peer reviews, especially with those colleagues that are allocating scarce resources across multiple sales territories.

As and when, you handover your sales territory, the incoming salesperson will be informed with a 'good heads up' on your organisation's relationship and sales strategies. It will save you both considerable time in the sales handover process. Likewise, if you are taking over a sales territory from a colleague, they will afford you the same courtesy and diligence to make the handover as smooth as possible.

I wish you 'good selling!'

End of main body of article

———

Thank you...

...For purchasing this booklet.

If you'd like further information about the variety of services I engage in, please visit these websites...

http://paulcburr.com/ ~ extensive and ethereal blog-site that combines business with ancient wisdom

http://www.facebook.com/PaulCBurr ~ over 16,000 followers

http://twitter.com/paulburr

Or mailto: doctapaul@paulcburr.com

Appendix: About me, Paul C Burr

Photo © Stephen Cotterell

I equip people to improve their effectiveness by 30%+ in a matter of weeks, sometimes days.

Business Client: *"I have worked with Paul periodically over the past 8 years to gain solutions to a number of people issues / opportunities. If you are looking for a Personal Coach to make a High Performer / High Performing Team even better (particularly a senior player) – I would not hesitate to recommend him."* - Sandra Ventre, Management Development Director, when with Reckitt Benckiser

Private Client: *"You have been so instrumental in the positive changes in my life, I set quite a few goals, and one by one my goals are being achieved, thanks to you, showing me how."* - Debbie (via Skype) Cape Town, South Africa.

Partial Client List... Accenture, Avery Dennison, Bevan Ashford, Bombardier, BP Marine, Cambridge Technology Partners, Castrol, Charles Burton (to become then European Amateur Natural Bodybuilding Champion), Cisco, Cotoco, CSC, Dept of Trade & Industry (private client), Dixons Group, DTZ, Erevena, Grace Construction, IBM, Microsoft, Newcastle City Council, Northumbria University, Prudential, Reckitt Benckiser, SHL, Staffware (now part of Tibco), United Biscuits, Xerox, Youthforce

The Skills and Passions in Me

Life doesn't get better by chance; it gets better by change.

And change is a journey that's two parts emotional to one part intellectual.

Most of us don't achieve what we set out to achieve at the first attempt. If the outcomes you sought were down to a purely intellectual exercise then you would have achieved them already - would you not? Whether you're a top or moderate performer (or underperforming right now) - every change you make in life is a journey, two parts emotional to one part intellectual. We are twice as likely to hold ourselves back because of self-imposed limiting beliefs we hold about ourselves, our organisation or customers, as opposed to intellectual problems. Put simply, I equip people to tackle challenging emotional journeys; to go beyond the limits to success they impose on themselves and others.

Corporate clients use me as a 'business coach', personal clients probably see me as more of an 'energy healer'. In both cases I help clients to cultivate and apply their innate willpower, imagination, courage and creativity to achieve the business and personal outcomes they seek.

I have over thirty-five years of B2B corporate sales and management experience, sixteen years of which overlap with my business and personal coaching work. I have a PhD in Statistics and a First Class Honours Degree in Mathematics. I'm qualified as a Master Practitioner in NLP, this/past life regression and hypnotherapy.

I give talks (and appear on talk shows) on selling, executive coaching, Neuro-Linguistic Programming (NLP), ancient wisdom, football and more ethereal subjects – sometimes to the same audience!

I write books, blogs and am now partway through a series of business articles based upon my own original research, experience and observations in corporate and small/medium sized businesses.

I study and practice ancient wisdom, astrology, casting runes, dowsing, the I Ching and the Tarot.

I love listening to music – rock, jazz, country... you name it. I sing a bit too.

I'm a passionate football fan of Newcastle United Football Club, in "Geordieland", in The North-East of England.

My Promise:

The material I use is powerful, very powerful. I know of nothing quicker or more effective. It's non-mainstream - which means you get non-mainstream results.

The Author in Me...

Quick Guides to Business, Volumes I - VI

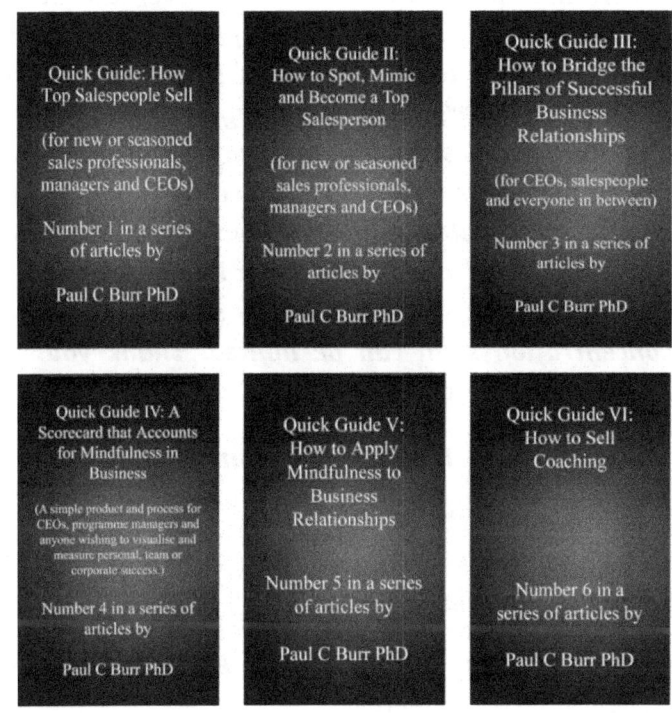

Quick Guide – How Top Salespeople Sell
"...a must read for both novice salespeople and the experienced...." - Author, Chiahou Zhang

"I loved it... it was great. I've encouraged many of my directors to buy a copy as it's very pertinent to my company" - paraphrased from a top performing B2B salesperson for a global IT Services organisation

"I work for a large American IT company, and can say this is a hugely powerful book to articulate what is required to get to Board level. To really understand what the CEO and C level executive summarise as valuable and impactful, and in a condensed easy-to-digest format, is phenomenal. I find Paul C Burr's style of writing easier to digest and apply in any sales situation; it crystallises where the true business value add is delivered and how you really have strategic partnerships. I have just got number 2 book and look forward to reading this with excitement - which is saying something as my concentration span can be limited. Thank you." - Amy Lambkin, 5-stars, book review

Quick Guide II - How to Spot, Mimic and Become a Top Salesperson

Quick Guide III - How to Bridge the Pillars of Successful Business Relationships

Quick Guide IV – A Scorecard that Accounts for Mindfulness in Business

Quick Guide V – How to Apply Mindfulness to Business Relationships

Quick Guide VI - How to Sell Coaching

Learn to Love and Be Loved in Return

"Uplifting: this is one of those books that arrives in your life at just the right time, when you need it most. The author is able to convey a very deep and meaningful message in an easy to read and understand format with a step by step guide on how to achieve this. The best type of love is unconditional and what better place to start than with yourself." - Rhedd, 5-stars, book review

2012: a twist in the tail, a novel with spiritual insights

"This is a compelling story for our troubled times. Paul C Burr writes with passion and compassion about moral uncertainties and the quest for salvation and spiritual fulfilment. Go with the flow, trust your inner-self and enjoy this humane and optimistic tale." - Professor John Ditch, York, UK.

"This is a gripping read - beautiful, insightful and very enjoyable. I found phrases and thoughts staying with me, and becoming part of my understanding of the world." - Caroline Eveleigh, *Getting to Excellent*

Defrag your Soul

"You should be proud of DYS Paul. I think it is amazing and I'm still thinking hard about what you've written." - Amanda Giles, Author

"DYS whispered to me, 'take heart, be aware, let your journey this far nourish your inner self to be at peace, to love and to shine as your journey continues'." - Penelope Walsh, Book Review

The Mystique to the Game of Life (and Unrequited Love)

"Revelatory - the Mystique to the Game of Life drew me in. I wanted to carry on reading as much as I wanted to stop and do the exercises! It struck a number of chords with me, and just through reading the book I became aware of some very important things - habits, conditioning, behaviours - that I needed to address to make my life and my relationships happier and healthier. The author has a way of writing that reaches deep down into your heart; it gets you in that feeling place. His writing is more than words on a page. It's more a guide that leads us to recognise, deal with and move on from whatever may be holding us back." - Amazon 5 star review.

For The Love of Lilith & How to Put Love into Practice (and Non-attach Yourself to It)

"For the Love of Lilith is a powerful tool to enhance the awareness, appreciation and enjoyment of living and loving in harmony. It is a book that can be used to strengthen and reinforce areas of my life and make sense of the non-sense that can accompany me in matters of the heart." - Amazon 5 star review.